This book belongs to

_____

This book is dedicated to my children - Mikey, Kobe, and Jojo.
A dream doesn't magically come true; it takes sweat equity.

978-1-63731-045-8 Printed and bound in the USA. First printing January 2021. ninjalifehacks.tv

Ninja Life Hacks®
by Mary Nhin

Hard-working Ninja

A Children's Book About Valuing a Hard Work Ethic

Ninja Life Hacks®
by Mary Nhin

Hi, I'm Hard-working Ninja and I'm not afraid of hard work.

There was a time, though, when I avoided anything remotely close to hard work.

My family and I had just gotten home from a brunch when we found Worry Ninja waiting at the door.

Soon after, the doorbell rang. It was Unplugged Ninja with a bunch of dogs.

I decided to go next door to visit my friend, Patient Ninja.

When I got home, my father asked me to help him paint the fence.

I picked up the paintbrush and ran it against the wood. I smiled with each stroke I made as I became lost in my thoughts. Then, Ambitious Ninja ran up to me.

As I continued to work, I thought about how dirty and dingy the old fence had looked. This new fence was beginning to breathe new life. It felt good to do something nice for the house and the yard. Just then, Creative Ninja stopped by to say hi.

As we got back to work, I thought about how the fence would be here for a long time. I felt proud to take my time to create something beautiful my family and the whole neighborhood might enjoy. Suddenly, Angry Ninja ran up.

As the sun was setting, I looked up to see everyone covered in paint.

I never knew hard work could be so fun and rewarding, I thought to myself.

Finally when all was done, I looked up at the fence.

It was a marvelous masterpiece, and I never felt more proud.

Remembering that hard work can be fun, rewarding, and character building could be your secret weapon in building a hard work ethic.

Check out the Hard-working Ninja lesson plans that contain fun activities to support the social, emotional lesson in this story at ninjalifehacks.tv!

I love to hear from my readers.
Write to me at info@ninjalifehacks.tv or send me mail at:

Mary Nhin
6608 N Western Avenue #1166
Oklahoma City, OK 73116

WORK HARD

Made in the USA
Columbia, SC
31 October 2024

45426176R00020